GET REAL!
WORKBOOK 2

GET REAL!

WORKBOOK 2

Miles Craven

MACMILLAN
English Language Teaching

To the student

This *Get Real! 2 Workbook* contains twelve practice units (24 lessons) designed to help you review important grammar and vocabulary contained in the Student Book units. Each unit gives you extra reading and writing practice using the language you have learned in class.

There is also a *Word Watch Plus* section which gives you extra vocabulary not included in the Student Book.

You can practice your pronunciation, too! This will help other people understand you more easily when you speak in English.

You can do these exercises on your own. The answers are in the Teacher's Guide and are photocopiable. So, you or your teacher can check your answers using this key.

If you do these Workbook exercises regularly, you will make more progress and you will be able to remember more of the English you cover in class. Try to complete each Workbook unit after you have finished a Student Book unit in class.

Enjoy learning English. Good luck!

Contents

	To the student	iv
1A	It's my birthday on July 3rd.	2
1B	What do people do at Christmas time?	4
2A	Why don't we have a party?	6
2B	I'll have soup, please.	8
3A	I like jazz a lot.	10
3B	I hate horror movies.	12
4A	How far is it to the airport?	14
4B	How high is Mount Everest?	16
5A	He went to Hollywood in 1996.	18
5B	I got engaged in January.	20
6A	How much rice do you want?	22
6B	How much paper do you recycle?	24
7A	It's bigger than China.	26
7B	I really like my new apartment.	28
8A	She's too young for me.	30
8B	This dress is not long enough.	32
9A	You should say you're sorry.	34
9B	I'm stressed.	36
10A	You can't smoke in the street.	38
10B	I have to get a visa.	40
11A	Have you ever tried Thai food?	42
11B	My computer's crashed.	44
12A	Have you bought your tickets yet?	46
12B	He's passed his driving test.	48
	Word Watch wordlist	50

1A It's my birthday on July 3rd.

1. Look at the pictures. Complete the sentences.

a. always
b. often
c. usually
d. sometimes
e. never

a. Amy ....*always gets presents*.. on her birthday.
   This year she's going to get some flowers from her boyfriend.

b. Amy .... on her birthday.
   This year she's going to go to a Chinese restaurant.

c. Amy .... on her birthday.
   But this year she's going to go to a karaoke club.

d. Amy .... on her birthday.
   But this year she isn't going to go to the movies.

e. Amy .... on her birthday.
   So she isn't going to work today!

2. Write answers to the questions about you.

a. What do you usually do on your birthday?
I usually go hiking.

b. What do you usually do on your birthday?
....

c. What do you never do on your birthday?
....

d. What do you sometimes do on your birthday?
....

e. What are you going to do this year on your birthday?
....

3. Complete the questions using the words in brackets with *going to*.

a. What *are you going to do* (you/do) on the weekend?
b. What movie .... (you/watch) tonight?
c. Where .... (you/go) tomorrow?
d. When .... (you/have) a dinner party?
e. What present .... (you/get) from your parents?

4. Circle the correct answers to complete the conversation.

Mike: Sam? It's Mike. Listen, it's my birthday next Sunday.
Sam: Wow! What a) (do you/**are you going to**) do?
Mike: Well, I usually b) (go/am going to go) to a restaurant with my family. But this year I c) ('ve/'m going to have) a party. Are you busy?
Sam: Hmm. I usually d) (visit/am going to visit) my parents on the weekend, but ...
Mike: Jane e) (is/is going to be) there!
Sam: OK! See you on Sunday!

What do people do at Christmas time?

1. Write the correct number next to each thing.

1. a parade   2. a float   3. firecrackers   4. fireworks   5. decorations

Now complete the sentences using these words.

~~go to~~   watch   light   put up   pull

a. Are you going to ......*go to*........ the parade this year?

b. Let's .... firecrackers!

c. I'm going to .... the fireworks.

d. Many people help to .... the float.

e. Lot's of people .... the decorations.

2. Read about the 4th of July. Answer the questions.

THE 4th OF JULY is a big celebration in the U.S. It's Independence Day. We have parties with our friends and put up red, white, and blue decorations. These are the colors of our flag. We eat hamburgers, have parades and light firecrackers. It's a great day!

a. What is the name of the festival? *Independence Day*

b. When is it? ....

c. What kind of decorations do people put up?
....

d. What do people eat? ....

e. What other things do they do? ....
....

3. Find eight words connected to festivals. Then write them.

L	A	N	A	F	I	L	J	A	D	M	E
F	I	R	E	C	R	A	C	K	E	R	S
F	P	R	E	S	E	N	T	S	C	A	G
R	A	L	P	L	N	T	S	D	O	O	P
A	R	A	C	F	I	E	C	M	R	I	O
D	A	U	A	B	T	R	L	P	A	T	N
P	D	R	N	P	R	N	O	C	T	I	A
F	E	M	D	P	C	S	F	R	I	S	L
I	T	F	L	O	A	T	S	X	O	N	T
R	I	F	E	S	R	O	T	F	N	A	Z
S	Q	Y	S	F	D	L	P	S	S	L	P
M	O	N	U	T	S	K	F	I	O	C	R

1. *parade*
2. ....
3. ....
4. ....
5. ....
6. ....
7. ....
8. ....

4. 🔊 **Practice your pronunciation. Listen and repeat these words. The stress is at the end.**

to<u>night</u>   pa<u>rade</u>   ex<u>change</u>   put <u>up</u>   put <u>on</u>   Chi<u>nese</u>

WORD WATCH PLUS

5. Match the actions on the left with the things on the right.

a. clean up — 1. to go to a party or celebration
b. blow out — 2. the turkey at Thanksgiving
c. host — 3. the table before a meal
d. carve — 4. after a party
e. get dressed up — 5. the birthday candles
f. set — 6. a dinner party

2A Why don't we have a party?

1. **Complete the conversation using the phrases below.**

| ~~Why don't we~~ | should we have | I'll phone | What should we | I'll buy |
| I'll go shopping | I'll put up | I'll wear | how about | I'll bake |

Catherine: a) *Why don't we* have a party?

Jennifer: That's a great idea! When b) .... one?

Catherine: Well, c) .... next Friday?
d) .... everyone tonight and ask them.

Jennifer: Yes, that's a good idea. And e) .... some drinks tomorrow.

Catherine: All right. What about food, though? f) .... have to eat?

Jennifer: Hmm. g) .... some pizzas. Everyone loves pizza.

Catherine: And h) .... some decorations. What should we wear?

Jennifer: Oh, that's easy. i) .... my new black dress. What about you?

Catherine: I guess j) .... for clothes tomorrow.

2. What decisions do Jennifer and Catherine make? Complete the notes.

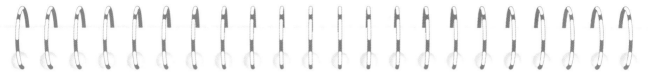

Catherine	Jennifer
a. *I'll phone everyone.*	d. ....
b.	e. ....
c.	f. ....

3. Match each sentence on the left with one on the right.

a. It's Jim's birthday on March 23rd.   1. OK. I'll reserve a table.
b. Why don't we go to a restaurant?   2. Why don't we have mushroom pizza?
c. Who will buy the food?   3. I will.
d. What should we eat?   4. OK. I'll call everyone.
e. I think we should invite a lot of people.   5. Why don't we have a party?

(a matches 5)

4. Put the words in the correct order to make sentences.

a. graduation / for / do / we / should / our / What
   What should we do for our graduation?

b. John / tomorrow / I'll / present / a / buy
   ....

c. we / a / Why / have / don't / party?
   ....

d. I'll / cocktails / some / make
   ....

e. six / table / for / reserve / o'clock / a / I'll
   ....

f. decorations / up / put / some / don't / we / Why
   ....

2B I'll have soup, please.

1. **Complete the dialogs using the words below.**

~~order~~	tart
dessert	salad
appetizer	shrimps
entree	

   Waiter: Are you ready to a) ....*order*.... ?
   Jane: Yes, thank you.
   Waiter: What would you like for your appetizer?
   Jane: I'll have b) .... , please.
   Waiter: And what about your entree?
   Jane: Ah! I'd like c) .... please.
   Waiter: And for dessert?
   Jane: I'll have lemon d) ....

   Waiter: And for you?
   Fred: I'll have soup for my e) .... , please.
   Waiter: And for your f) .... ?
   Fred: Hmm. I think I'll have omelette.
   Waiter: A very good choice. What about g) .... ?
   Fred: Oh, that's easy! I'll have ice cream, please.

   Now unscramble the words to find more dishes.

   a. kccenih rycru ....*chicken curry*........
   b. ledosno ....
   c. truif atrt ....
   d. tfou ....

2. **Read the conversation and write the order.**

   A: Are you ready to order?
   B: Yes, please.
   A: What would you like for your appetizer?
   B: I'm hungry! I'll have onion soup and tomato salad, please.
   A: And for your entree?
   B: Let me see. I'd like chicken.
   A: And what about dessert?
   B: Oh, that's easy! I'll have chocolate ice cream, please. And fresh fruit!

   Appetizer
   a. ....*onion soup*........
   b. ....

   Entree
   c. ....

   Dessert
   d. ....
   e. ....

3. **Write the dishes below in the correct column.**

   ~~soup~~   chicken curry   noodles with fried tofu   ice cream
   lemon tart   grilled shrimps   small salad   fruit tart   omelette

   Appetizers
   a. ....*soup*........
   b. ....

   Entrees
   c. ....
   d. ....
   e. ....
   f. ....

   Desserts
   g. ....
   h. ....
   i. ....

4. 🔊 **Practice your pronunciation. Listen and repeat these words. The stress is at the beginning.**

   <u>le</u>mon   <u>en</u>tree   <u>chi</u>cken   <u>to</u>fu   <u>noo</u>dles   <u>mush</u>rooms

WORD WATCH PLUS

5. **Write *M* (meat), *V* (vegetarian), or *S* (seafood).**

   a. ...*M*... roast lamb
   b. .... leek and onion pie
   c. .... haddock and chips
   d. .... buffalo burger
   e. .... broccoli and cheese gratin
   f. .... clam chowder

3A I like jazz a lot.

1. **Complete the sentences.**

   crazy about = ✓✓✓
   love = ✓✓
   like = ✓
   don't like = ✗
   hate = ✗✗
   can't stand = ✗✗✗

   Hey, Simon. Do you like old movies?

   No, I can't stand them. How about you, Tracy?

   Oh, I love movies!

	Simon	Sharon	Tracy
old movies	✗✗✗	✗✗✗	✓✓
rock music	✓✓	✗	✗
golf	✗	✓	✓
computer games	✓✓✓	✗✗	✓✓✓
soccer	✗✗	✓✓	✗
karaoke	✓	✓✓✓	✗✗✗

   Simon a) ......can't stand...... old movies, but Tracy b) ......loves...... them.
   Tracy c) .... rock music, but she d) .... golf.
   Sharon e) .... soccer, and she's f) .... karaoke.
   Tracy and Sharon g) .... golf, but Simon h) .... it.
   Simon i) .... karaoke, but Tracy j) .... it.
   Simon and Tracy are k) .... computer games, but Sharon
   l) .... them.

2. **Match the sentences on the left with the ones on the right.**

   a. Simon can't stand old movies.   1. No, he doesn't.
   b. Does Tracy hate rock music?   2. So is Simon.
   c. Is Simon crazy about golf?   3. Yes, she does.
   d. Sharon likes golf.   4. So does Tracy.
   e. Does Simon like soccer?   5. Neither can Sharon.
   f. Tracy is crazy about computer games.   6. No, he isn't.

3. Complete the dialogs using the phrases below.

~~No, I don't.~~   I'd love to!   So am I.
I'm crazy about it.   Neither do I.   I can't stand it.

Reporter: Do you like soccer?
Carol Star: a) *No, I don't.* But I'm crazy about golf.
Reporter: b) .... I practice every Sunday. How about karaoke? Do you like karaoke?
Carol Star: c) .... So no, I never go to karaoke clubs.
Reporter: d) .... What about music? Do you like jazz?
Carol Star: e) ....
Reporter: Hey, would you like to go to the jazz concert this weekend?
Carol Star: f) ....

4. Reply to the statements. Give real answers.

a. I love soccer! *So do I./I don't.*
b. I love cooking! ....
c. I don't like golf. ....
d. I like swimming. ....
e. I'm crazy about action movies. ....
f. I really hate spiders. ....

3B   I hate horror movies.

1. **Write the number of each type of movie next to the matching poster.**

   1. an animated movie
   2. a romance
   3. a science fiction movie
   4. a comedy
   5. an action movie
   6. a horror movie

2. **Read this movie guide. Find adjectives that describe the movie.**

My Life in Pictures is a comedy with Billy Star and Norma Angel. It's a great movie and it's funny and romantic. A young man leaves his hometown at the age of 13 and travels around the world. He has lots of adventures. It is an exciting movie, and is interesting enough for the whole family. It's not scary, so don't worry about the kids! And it isn't boring!
★★★★★

The movie is:
a. ……great……
b. ……………
c. ……………
d. ……………
e. ……………

The movie isn't:
f. ……………
g. ……………

3. **Complete the crossword.**

   1. I'm crazy about s____ f____ movies. "Star Wars" is great!
   2. I really like action movies because they're so e____ .
   3. I don't like r____ movies at all. They're boring.
   4. "Toy Story II" is a great a____ movie.
   5. I can't stand h____ movies because they're too scary.
   6. Comedies are f____ . They always make me laugh.
   7. My sister likes documentaries because she says they're i____ .

4. 🔊 **Practice your pronunciation. Listen and repeat these sentences. The stress is on *I* when it's at the end of the sentence.**

I love Italian food!	So do <u>I</u>.
I don't like golf.	Neither do <u>I</u>.
I'm crazy about jazz.	So am <u>I</u>.
I can't stand Kung Fu movies.	Neither can <u>I</u>.

WORD WATCH PLUS

5. **Write the words below in the correct column.**

   ~~violent~~   critic   slow   thriller   western   director

movie people	kinds of movie	adjectives
a.	c.	e. ......*violent*......
b.	d.	f. ....

13

4A How far is it to the airport?

1. **Complete the dialog using the words below.**

   ~~Can~~   costs   long   do   far   much

   A: Hello. a) ......*Can*...... I help you?
   B: Well, I'd like to go to the Grand Hotel.
      How b) .... is it, please?
   A: It's about five kilometers from here.
      It's on East Street.
   B: I see. How c) .... I get there?
   A: Well, you can take the bus. The bus stop
      is across the road. Or the subway.
   B: How d) .... does it take by bus?
   A: By bus, about twenty minutes. By subway it
      takes about five minutes.
   B: Oh, and how e) .... does it cost?
   A: The bus f) .... $1.25. The subway is
      $1.50. Oh, look! There's a bus now.
   B: Great! I'll get the bus. Thanks for your help!

2. **Complete the questions.**

   a. A: How ....*do I get*............ to the Grand Hotel?
      B: You can take the bus or the subway.

   b. A: How .... to the Grand Hotel?
      B: It's about five kilometers.

   c. A: How .... take by bus?
      B: It takes about twenty minutes.

   d. A: How .... cost?
      B: The bus costs about $2.00.

   e. A: How .... take by subway?
      B: It takes about five minutes.

3. Match the questions on the left with the answers on the right.

a. How far is it to your office from here?
b. How much does it cost by taxi?
c. How long does it take by train?
d. How do I get to the Rockefeller Center?
e. Can I help you?
f. How much does a round-trip ticket cost?

1. Yes, please. I'd like some information.
2. A round-trip ticket costs $23.00.
3. It's two kilometers.
4. A taxi costs around $10.00.
5. Take the number 10 bus. It's three stops.
6. It takes about twenty minutes.

4. Look at the information. Write the questions.

	Distance	Transportation	Cost	Time
The Art Museum	5 kilometers	subway	$5.50	5 minutes
Don's Diner	7 kilometers	bus	$8.00	12 minutes
Nightclub Trendy	12 kilometers	taxi	$25.00	15 minutes
The Shopping Center	2 kilometers	subway	$3.50	2 minutes

a. A: *How far is it to Don's Diner?*
   B: It's 7 kilometers.

b. A: I want to go to Nightclub Trendy. ....
   B: It's $25.00.

c. A: ....
   B: It takes five minutes by subway.

d. A: ....
   B: Take the subway. It takes two minutes.

e. A: ....
   B: It's 12 kilometers.

f. A: I want to go to the Art Museum. ....
   B: It costs $5.50.

4B How high is Mount Everest?

1. **Look at the map. Write the number of each thing in the correct place on the map.**

    1. a waterfall
    2. a volcano
    3. a gorge
    4. a hiking trail
    5. the Pacific Ocean

2. **Read the diary. Answer the questions.**

   Dear Diary,
   Hawaii is amazing! Yesterday, we visited a volcano called Mauna Loa. It's 4,169 meters high. Then we saw a beautiful waterfall called Akaka Falls. It falls into a gorge that is 120 meters deep.

   This morning, we went swimming in the Pacific Ocean. It's 30 degrees C! Perfect! Tomorrow we are going to go hiking in Volcanoes National Park. The hiking trail is 10 kilometers long and will take three hours.

   Hawaii is called "the big island." How big is it? Our guide says that the island is 10,443 square kilometers.

   a. How high is Mauna Loa? *It's 4,169 meters high.*
   b. How long is the hiking trail? ....
   c. How deep is the gorge? ....
   d. How warm is the Pacific Ocean? ....
   e. How big is Hawaii? ....

3. Find the words for seven geographical features. Then write them.

D	E	S	V	O	L	S	P	R	O	C	E
O	C	D	E	S	E	R	T	H	I	B	L
Y	B	H	U	I	V	I	E	R	C	W	T
U	V	B	U	D	O	V	E	G	H	W	A
V	O	L	T	P	O	E	N	P	S	A	N
O	L	I	P	S	P	R	I	N	G	T	M
L	C	P	A	H	C	C	G	A	B	E	L
O	A	G	O	R	G	E	A	A	C	R	P
C	N	C	O	Q	T	Y	D	R	V	F	G
S	O	U	Y	C	H	C	X	G	S	A	H
M	C	O	C	E	A	N	A	W	R	L	K
H	O	T	S	P	R	I	N	G	S	L	L

1. *desert*
2. ....
3. ....
4. ....
5. ....
6. ....
7. ....

4. 🔊 **Practice your pronunciation. Listen and repeat these words. Is the stress at the beginning or at the end? Write each word in the correct column.**

~~desert~~ ~~degrees~~ New York   river   July   airport

desert	*degrees*
....	....
....	....
....	....

WORD WATCH PLUS

5. Complete the sentences using the words below.

~~continent~~   earthquake   island   iceberg   tornado   mountain range

a. Asia is a .... *continent.* ....
b. An .... is land surrounded by water.
c. A .... is a very strong wind.
d. The Rockies are a ....
e. When the earth moves it is called an ....
f. An .... is a large piece of ice in the ocean.

5A He went to Hollywood in 1996.

1. **Complete the conversation using the verbs in brackets.**

Mark: What are you reading?
Julie: It's a book about Bruce Lee.
Mark: Are you a Bruce Lee fan?
Julie: Oh, yes. Did you know he a) ....*lived*........ (live) in California?
Mark: No, but I know he b) .... (be) a famous action movie star.
Julie: He c) .... (start) to make movies when he was six. And when he was 32 he d) .... (make) "The Way of the Dragon," his last movie.
Mark: e) .... he ever .... (go) to Hollywood?
Julie: f) Yes, many times. He .... (go) to Hollywood to work in TV.

2. **Write the sentences as negatives.**

   a. Bruce Lee lived in Australia. ....*Bruce Lee didn't live in Australia.*........
   b. He wrote songs. ....
   c. He was a famous golf player. ....
   d. Bruce Lee went to London. ....
   e. He made movies in New York. ....

3. Look at the timeline and complete the story.

Year:	1940	1941	1946	1958	1966	1973
Age:	0	1	6	18	26	32
	is born in San Francisco	moves to Hong Kong	makes first movie	wins dance contest	starts working in TV in the USA	makes last movie

a) ......*When*...... he was one, he b) .... from San Francisco to Hong Kong. In c) .... , he made his first movie. In 1958, he d) .... a dance contest. When he e) .... 26, he started working in TV in the U.S. In 1973, he f) .... his last movie. He was 32.

4. Put the words in the correct order to make questions.

a. movie / When / first / did / his / Bruce Lee / make
  When did Bruce Lee make his first movie?

b. Did / live / Hong Kong / he / in
  ....

c. famous / he / Was / 1965 / in / a / movie / star
  ....

d. last / he / Where / make / movie / did / his
  ....

e. go / he / When / did / Hollywood / to
  ....

f. make / he / Did / movies / ago / time / a / long
  ....

19

5B I got engaged in January.

1. Write the number of each sentence next to the correct person.

1. I failed my exams yesterday.
2. I'm moving to a new apartment.
3. I separated from my partner a few weeks ago.
4. We got engaged last month.

2. Read the letter. Then write T (true) or F (false).

Dear Sue,

Hi. As you know, Mark and I got married last month. I'm sorry you missed it, but here is a photo. It was a great day. And he graduated from university, so we had a lot to celebrate. We're moving to a new apartment next month. And I got a promotion a few weeks ago! I know you moved into a new apartment last week. How is it? And how is your new job?

Lots of love,

Jane

a. Jane got engaged last month.   F
b. Mark got a promotion last month.
c. Jane and Mark are moving to a new apartment.
d. Sue moved into a new apartment last week.
e. Sue is starting a new job soon.

3. **Complete the crossword.**

   1. A: My dog died last night.
      B: Oh, dear. I'm s____ to hear that.

   2. A: I'm so happy! I got e____ last week.
      B: Congratulations!

   3. A: Sara is m____ to a new apartment soon.
      B: That's good news.

   4. A: My brother is getting m____ on Saturday.
      B: Is he? Congratulations!

   5. A: Did you g____ from university?
      B: No, I didn't. I left school when I was sixteen.

   6. A: I was b____ on Friday the 13th.
      B: Oh, dear.

   7. A: I really want to get a p____ this year.
      B: Good luck!

   8. A: I'm starting a new job on Monday.
      B: G____ l____!

   3across: m o v i n g

4. 🌐 **Practice your pronunciation. Listen and repeat these words. The stress is at the beginning, but one word is different. Circle it.**

   graduate   Wimbledon   Hollywood   separate   promotion   waterfall

---

WORD WATCH PLUS

5. **Write these phrases in the correct place.**

   ~~take up exercise~~   get divorced   go bald   quit smoking   put on weight   get a raise

   Good changes
   a. ....*take up exercise*....
   b. ....
   c. ....

   Bad changes
   d. ....
   e. ....
   f. ....

21

6A How much rice do you want?

1. Put these things in the correct column.

much	many
a. *beef*	d. ....
b.	e. ....
c.	f. ....

2. Mary and Tim are packing for a camping trip. Complete the dialog using the words below.

~~much~~   a lot   many   a little   none   much

Tim: How a) .....*much*..... rice do you want?
Mary: Just one bag. Thanks.
Tim: How about beef? How b) .... beef do you want?
Mary: c) ...., thanks. I don't eat meat. I need carrots.
Tim: How d) .... do you want?
Mary: e) .... I love carrots! And do we have butter?
Tim: Yes, we do.
Mary: I'd like f) .... butter, please.

3. Complete the questions using *much* or *many*. Then match the answers.

a. How .....*much*..... rice does Mary want?   1. A little.
b. How .... beef does she want?   2. None.
c. How .... carrots does she want?   3. A lot.
d. How .... butter does she want?   4. Just one bag.

4. Write questions using *How much* or *How many*.

a. I'd like some coffee.
   How much would you like?

b. I'd like some tomatoes.
   ....

c. I'd like some carrots.
   ....

d. I'd like some curry.
   ....

e. I'd like some soup.
   ....

f. I'd like some apples.
   ....

How much paper do you recycle?

1. How can this family help the environment? Write the number of each phrase in the correct box.

1. Keep the streets clean.
2. Recycle cans and bottles.
3. Save gasoline.
4. Save water.
5. Save electricity.

2. Read the report and complete the notes.

Report:

They're using a lot of electricity and water. They're throwing away a lot of aluminum cans and glass bottles, and they aren't recycling any paper. They're throwing away three bags of garbage. They're going to school by car, so they're using a lot of gasoline.

Throwing away a lot of
a. *aluminum cans*
b. ....
c. ....

Using a lot of
d. ....
e. ....
f. ....

24

3. **Unscramble the letters to find eight words.**

   a. maumnuil .... *aluminum* ....
   b. glaneois ....
   c. lircngeyc ....
   d. gegabar ....
   e. atspcil ....
   f. etritylccie ....
   g. htsra nacs ....
   h. repap ....

4. 🔊 **Practice your pronunciation. Listen and repeat these words. The stress is in the middle, but one word is different. Circle it.**

   recycle   potatoes   gasoline   banana   Sahara   Pacific

WORD WATCH PLUS

5. **Match the words with the correct definitions.**

   1. ozone layer   3. global warming
   2. acid rain   4. smog

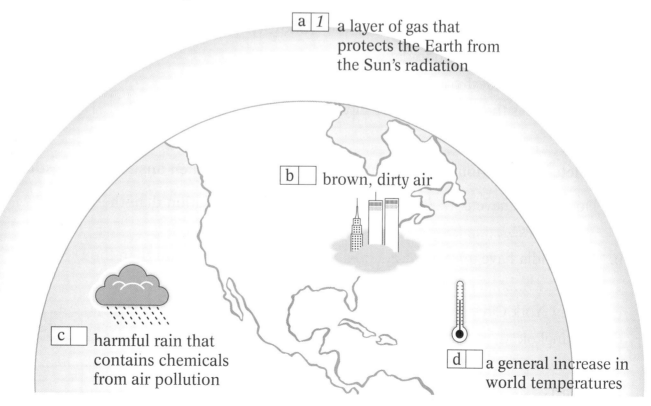

a. [1] a layer of gas that protects the Earth from the Sun's radiation

b. [ ] brown, dirty air

c. [ ] harmful rain that contains chemicals from air pollution

d. [ ] a general increase in world temperatures

7A It's bigger than China.

1. Look at this information. Write T (true) or F (false) for the statements below.

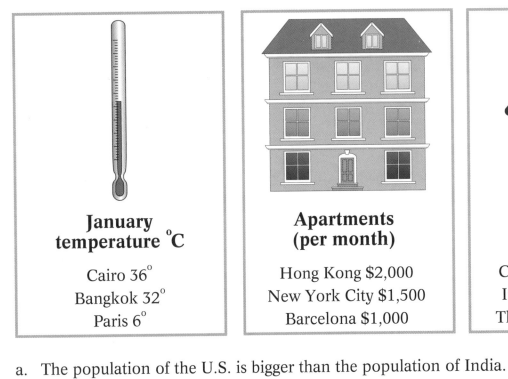

January temperature °C	Apartments (per month)	Population
Cairo 36°	Hong Kong $2,000	China 1,250,000,000
Bangkok 32°	New York City $1,500	India 1,000,000,000
Paris 6°	Barcelona $1,000	The U.S. 272,000,000

a. The population of the U.S. is bigger than the population of India. F
b. Cairo is the hottest city in January.
c. Barcelona is more expensive than New York City.
d. China has the biggest population.
e. Paris is the coldest city in January.
f. Barcelona is the most expensive city.

2. Complete the questions using the adjectives in brackets. Then answer the questions.

a. Does China have a ......*bigger*...................... (big) population than the U.S.?
   ..*Yes, it does.*..................
b. Does India have a .... (small) population than the U.S.?
   ....
c. Is New York City .... (expensive) than Barcelona? ....
d. Is Bangkok .... (hot) than Cairo in January? ....
e. Is New York City .... (expensive) city? ....
f. Is Paris .... (cold) city in January? ....

26

3. **Complete the sentences using the adjectives in brackets.**

   a. Living in Tokyo is even ...*more expensive than*... (expensive) living in New York City.
   b. Canada is huge! It's .... (big) than the U.S.
   c. I think soccer is .... (exciting) than baseball. Baseball is boring.
   d. Hawaii is .... (stressful) than New York City. Hawaii is more relaxed!
   e. Is it true that Mount Everest is .... (high) mountain in the world?
   f. Spain is .... (hot) than Britain in the summer.

4. **Complete the conversation using the verbs in brackets.**

Adam: Let's go to Hawaii on vacation this year! We'll have a great time.

Jan: Well, I think France is a) ......*more interesting*...... (interesting) than Hawaii. There is so much to see.

Adam: But a beach in Hawaii is b) .... (relaxing) than France. And it's c) .... (expensive). We don't have a lot of money.

Jan: I know. But they say Paris is d) .... (romantic) city in the world! I want a e) .... (exciting) vacation than last year, when we just stayed at home.

Adam: I know, but a trip to Hawaii is f) .... (stressful) than traveling to Europe. I want a g) .... (peaceful) vacation than we had last year in New York City.

27

7B I really like my new apartment.

1. Look at the pictures. What words describe each home?

a. modern [1]   c. old-fashioned ☐   e. messy ☐
b. dark   ☐   d. neat   ☐   f. bright ☐

2. Read the letter. Complete the notes.

Dear Sue,

Well, Mark and I moved into a new apartment yesterday. It is more beautiful and more spacious than our old apartment, and it is brighter too. And it's more modern, and we like that. Our old apartment was very old-fashioned. The neighborhood is a lot noisier, though, as we are near a main road. Anyway, nothing is perfect! Please come and visit us soon. We're looking forward to seeing you here.

Love and best wishes,
Jane

Jane and Mark's new apartment

Good points

a. ......*more beautiful*......
b. ....
c. ....
d. ....

Bad point

e. ....

3. Write the opposites of the adjectives in the puzzle. What extra word can you find?

1. bright
2. noisy
3. stressful
4. clean
5. dark
6. neat
7. old-fashioned
8. peaceful
9. messy

4. 🔊 Practice your pronunciation. Listen and repeat these words. Do they begin with /t/ or /d/? Write each word in the correct column.

~~dark~~   ~~tall~~   travel   transportation   die   deep

/d/	/t/
dark	tall
....	....
....	....

WORD WATCH PLUS

5. Put the words in the box in the correct column.

~~comfortable~~   inconvenient   shabby   dangerous   convenient   cozy

Good points
a. .... *comfortable* ....
b. ....
c. ....

Bad points
d. ....
e. ....
f. ....

8A   She's too young for me.

1. Look at the picture. Complete the conversations using *too* or *enough* and the words below.

   ~~young~~   quiet   thin   old   tall

Joy: What do you think of Dave?
Gina: Dave is a) ......*too young*............
Joy: Mike is nice.
Gina: Mike? He's not b) ....
Joy: What about John?
Gina: John is c) ....
Joy: I think Brian likes you!
Gina: Brian is not d) ....
Joy: I think Sam is nice.
Gina: Sam is e) ....

2. Write answers for these questions.

   A: Why don't you do karaoke?
   B: Because I'm a) ....*too shy*.............. (shy).
      And I'm b) ....*not good enough*............... (good).
   A: Why aren't you a movie star?
   B: Because I'm c) .... (short).
      And I'm d) .... (good-looking).
   A: Why don't you marry Steve?
   B: Because he's e) .... (shy) for me.
      He's f) .... (outgoing).

30

3. Put the words in the correct order to make sentences.

a. shoes / big / My / too / new / are
   My new shoes are too big.

b. me / for / old / too / He's
   ....

c. romantic / isn't / Sam / enough / me /for
   ....

d. apartment / big / This / isn't / enough
   ....

e. can't / it's / I / because / go / too / expensive / skiing
   ....

f. old / drive / I / can't / enough / not / I'm / because
   ....

4. Write replies to disagree with these sentences.

a. I think Rob is too outgoing.
   Really? I don't think so. He's not outgoing enough.

b. I think London is a really exciting city.
   Really? I don't think so. ....

c. I think this restaurant is really good.
   Really? I don't think so. ....

d. I think you're new apartment is big!
   Really? I don't think so. ....

e. I think your boyfriend is so romantic.
   Really? I don't think so. ....

f. I think it's too hot here.
   Really? I don't think so. ....

8B This dress is not long enough.

1. **Unscramble the letters to find the clothes. Then number each item of clothing in the picture.**

   1. awteers .....*sweater*.....
   2. rihts ....
   3. atnsp ....
   4. kirst ....
   5. akcjet ....
   6. souelb ....

2. **Read the note. Complete the forms.**

   Returns Form
   CUSTOMER:
   a) ......*Miss Jones*......
   ITEM:
   b) ....
   PROBLEM:
   c) ....

   Returns Form
   CUSTOMER:
   d) ....
   ITEM:
   e) ....*pants*........
   PROBLEM:
   f) ....

   Returns Form
   CUSTOMER:
   g) ....
   ITEM:
   h) ....
   PROBLEM:
   i) ......*too tight*......

   Note

   Michelle,

   Some customers have problems with the clothes they bought. I didn't have time to fill in the Returns Forms. Can you do it? Miss Jones returned the white blouse because she said it was too baggy. Then Mr. Smith came in and said that his pants weren't long enough. Finally, about ten minutes ago Mrs. Green returned a skirt she bought. It is too tight.

   Thanks a lot.

   Mike, Customer Services

3. **Find ten items of clothing or adjectives. Then write them.**

K	S	K	I	R	T	M	A	H	F	S
N	B	B	A	G	G	Y	E	B	A	H
H	I	L	O	K	P	N	X	B	S	I
E	X	O	M	I	A	N	P	B	H	B
B	A	U	B	L	N	J	E	N	I	I
B	N	S	N	B	T	N	N	O	O	C
C	H	E	A	P	S	D	S	M	N	A
S	W	E	A	T	E	R	I	B	A	B
S	H	U	R	Y	S	E	V	E	B	E
S	H	I	R	T	B	S	E	R	L	V
A	L	R	I	N	L	S	C	O	E	T

1. ....skirt....
2. ....
3. ....
4. ....
5. ....
6. ....
7. ....
8. ....
9. ....
10. ....

4. 🔊 **Practice your pronunciation. Listen and repeat these words. Do they begin with /p/ or /b/? Write each word in the correct column.**

~~pants~~ ~~baggy~~ bottles peaceful beautiful population

/p/	/b/
pants	baggy
....	....
....	....

WORD WATCH PLUS

5. **Complete the paragraph using the words and phrases below.**

~~size~~   fitting room   try them on   put on   fit   took off

I went into a clothes store yesterday and saw a great pair of jeans. Luckily, they had my a) ....size.... so I decided to b) .... I went into the c) .... and d) .... my jacket and pants. When I e) .... the jeans I was very happy. They were a good f) ....

33

9A You should say you're sorry.

1. Write the number of each sentence in the correct place to complete the dialog.

1. You should go home and study.
2. Why don't you ask her for a date?
3. Perhaps you'd better get a part-time job.
4. Perhaps you'd better forget Julie.
5. Why don't you go to a doctor?

Peter: I really like Julie.
Koji: a) ...2...
Peter: I asked her three times. She said no every time.
Koji: Oh dear. b) ....
Peter: I have another problem. I have an exam tomorrow.
Koji: c) ....
Peter: But I have a stomachache.
Koji: d) ....
Peter: I don't like the doctor. And I don't have any money.
Koji: e) ....
Peter: Maybe. But the salary is never high enough.

2. Complete the dialogs using *should* and the words in brackets.

a. A: I never have any money.
    B: Oh, dear. You .... *should find a job* .... (job / a / find)

b. A: I feel terrible.
    B: Oh, dear. You .... (a / go / doctor / to)

c. A: I never do well in exams.
    B: Oh, dear. You .... (homework / do / your)

d. A: I am always late for class.
    B: Oh, dear. You .... (take / train / the)

e. A: My parents are mad at me.
    B: Oh, dear. You .... (you're / sorry / say)

3. These people want some advice. Complete the sentences using the phrases below with *better*, *should*, or *don't you*.

~~go to bed earlier~~   say you're sorry   tell your teacher   go to parties more often

a. Sue, perhaps you'd *better go to bed earlier.*
b. Patrick, why ....
c. Joe, I think you'd ....
d. Sally, why ....

4. Look at the picture and give James some advice.

a. James *should be neat.* (be neat)
b. He *shouldn't be messy.* (be messy)
c. James .... (exercise)
d. He .... (smoke)
e. James .... (study more)
f. He .... (read comics)

9B I'm stressed.

1. **This is the Edams family. What problems do they have? Complete the sentences using the words below.**

   ~~indigestion~~   stressed   overweight   exhausted

   a. Jill has ....*indigestion*..................
   b. Mrs. Edams is ....
   c. Mr. Edams is ....
   d. Mark is ....

   Now match each person with the correct advice.

   1. You should go on a diet. ...*Mark*..........
   2. You should have a massage. ....
   3. You should eat more slowly. ....
   4. You should sleep more. ....

2. **Read this information. Write T (true) or F (false) for each statement.**

   a. You should exercise in the morning only. [F]
   b. Coffee gives you insomnia. ☐
   c. Smoking increases stress. ☐
   d. You should think about your problems a lot. ☐
   e. You should sleep more than eight hours. ☐

   ### A healthy life!

   Take some advice for a stress-free, long life:

   ★ Don't drink too much coffee, especially late at night, or you'll sleep badly.
   ★ Don't smoke. Smokers are more stressed than non-smokers.
   ★ Sleep seven or eight hours a night. But not more, or you'll become tired.
   ★ Exercise regularly. Work out in the morning or at night.
   ★ Don't worry too much about your problems.

3. Match the words on the left with the sentences on the right.

a. insomnia
b. pimples
c. indigestion
d. overweight
e. sunburn
f. exhausted

1. Your skin is red after being in the sun.
2. You have spots on your face.
3. You are very, very tired.
4. You can't sleep.
5. You have a stomachache.
6. You are too heavy.

4. 🔊 Practice your pronunciation. Listen and repeat these sentences. Suggestions usually have a falling intonation.

Perhaps you'd better go on a diet.

Why don't you get a job?

You should say you're sorry.

Why don't you go to a doctor?

WORD WATCH PLUS

5. Write the number in the correct place in the picture.

1. I have a nosebleed.
2. I have a concussion.
3. I grazed my knee.
4. I broke my arm.
5. I have a bruise on my leg.
6. I twisted my ankle.

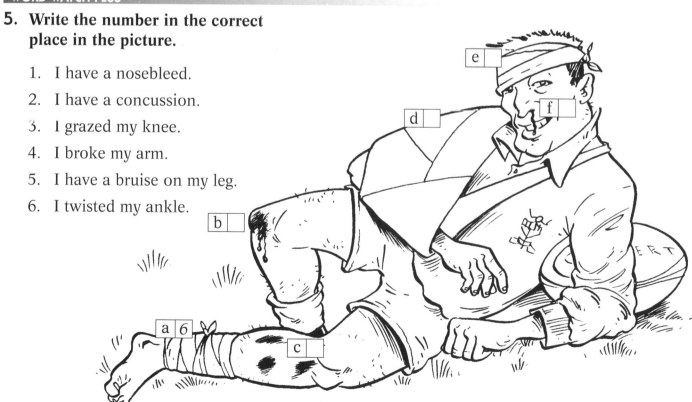

10A You can't smoke in the street.

1. Look at the picture. Complete the conversations using the words below.

~~can~~   don't have to   can't   have to   has to

a. Man: What about our bags?
   Woman: No problem. You ......*can*.......... leave your bags there.

b. Alice: It's free!
   Tina: Great! We .... pay, then.

c. Jane: My son has a new job. He .... leave home at 6:00 a.m. now.
   Doris: That's early.

d. Man: Hey! You .... sit here.
   Woman: Oh, sorry.

e. Man: We .... buy tickets, Fred.

2. Look at exercise 1 again. Complete the questions.

a. A: ..*Can they*... leave their bags?
   B: Yes. They can leave them in the luggage lockers.

b. A: .... pay?
   B: No, they don't. It's free!

c. A: What time .... her son .... leave home?
   B: He has to leave home at 6 a.m.

d. A: .... sit on the grass?
   B: No, they can't. The sign says "Keep off the grass."

e. A: .... buy tickets?
   B: Yes, they do.

3. Complete the sentences using *have to* or *has to*.

a. When I'm busy I ...*have to*... work overtime.
b. Sara .... go to the dentist. She has a toothache.
c. In England you .... drive on the left side of the road.
d. They .... study hard every night.
e. Oh no! The bus is late and we .... be at work in five minutes.
f. Paul .... leave now. He has a meeting.

DRIVE ON LEFT

4. Put the words in the correct order to make sentences.

a. work / to / I / at / have / start / seven
   I have to start work at seven.

b. get / don't / to / I / have / early / up
   ....

c. We / here / wear / our / can't / shoes
   ....

d. English / homework / has / to / his / again / do / Tom
   ....

e. in / You / go / can
   ....

10B I have to get a visa.

1. Write the words from the picture next to the correct verb.

a. buy some ......*traveler's checks*..........
b. declare your ....
c. show your ....
   and ....
d. check in your ....
e. book a ....

2. Read the conversation. Complete the notes.

A: I want to go to France. Do I have to get a visa?

B: No, you don't.

A: Good. What about vaccinations? Do I have to get any vaccinations?

B: No. But you will have to show your passport at the airport.

A: OK. How long can I stay in France?

B: You can stay for four months.

A: And can you book my hotel?

B: Yes, no problem.

Country: a) ......*France*......

Visa required?: b) ....

Maximum length of stay: c) ....

Vaccinations required?: d) ....

Can travel agent book hotel?: e) ....

3. **Find words connected with air travel in the puzzle. What extra word can you find?**

   1. Go through ____
   2. Get some ____
   3. ____ your baggage
   4. Buy some ____
   5. Declare your ____ goods
   6. Show your ____

4. 🎧 **Practice your pronunciation. Listen and repeat these words. Do they begin with /v/ or /f/? Write each word in the correct column.**

   ~~vaccination~~ ~~formal~~ visa volcano fashionable Philippines

/v/	/f/
vaccination	*formal*
....	....
....	....

WORD WATCH PLUS

5. **Match the words on the left with the ones on the right.**

   a. non-smoking   1. luggage
   b. take   2. flight
   c. overhead   3. locker
   d. hand   4. allowance
   e. baggage   5. off
   f. economy   6. class

11A Have you ever tried Thai food?

1. **Complete the conversation using the verbs below.**

   ~~be~~ spend do have work travel try

   Reporter: Tell me, Miss Divine, have you ever a) ...*been*... to Europe?
   Ms. Divine: Oh, yes. Many times. I've b) .... all over Europe.
   Reporter: Have you ever c) .... with Robert di Niro?
   Ms. Divine: Yes, I have. We worked together on "The Manager." I've d) .... a lot of time with Robert. He's my good friend.
   Reporter: Miss Divine, have you ever e) .... any special exercises to keep fit?
   Ms. Divine: I f) .... yoga last year, but I didn't like it. It was boring.
   Reporter: Have you ever g) .... a massage?
   Ms. Divine: Of course! I have one every day!

2. **Read the interview again. Write questions for these answers.**

   a. *Has Miss Divine ever been to Europe?*
      Yes, she has. She's been to Europe many times.

   b. ....
      Yes, she has. They worked together on "The Manager."

   c. ....
      Yes, she has. Robert is her good friend.

   d. ....
      Yes, she has. She tried yoga last year.

   e. ....
      Yes, she has. She has one every day.

3. **Make questions using the words in brackets. Then give real answers for you.**

   a. *Have you ever lived in the U.K.?* .... (you / live / U.K.)
   b. .... (you / eat / frog legs)
   c. .... (you / work / a restaurant)
   d. .... (you / fail / an exam)
   e. .... (you / travel / by plane)
   f. .... (you / do / yoga)

   a. *Yes, I have.* or *No, I haven't.*
   b. ....
   c. ....
   d. ....
   e. ....
   f. ....

4. **Write sentences that disagree.**

   a. Tom has been to France. (Germany)
      No, he hasn't. He's been to Germany.

   b. Mary has eaten Spanish food. (Italian food)
      ....
      ....

   c. James has done tai chi. (yoga)
      ....
      ....

   d. Susan has worked in a bank. (post office)
      ....
      ....

   e. Mark has lived in the U.S. (Australia)
      ....

   f. Peter has tried chicken feet. (frog legs)
      ....

11B My computer's crashed.

1. Write the words below in the correct place.

   the ~~printer~~   the screen   the mouse   a floppy disk   the keyboard   the monitor

   a. *the printer*
   b. ....
   c. ....
   d. ....
   e. ....
   f. ....

2. Read the memo. Match the words on the left with the words on the right.

   ACE Computing Company

   MEMO

   Jack,
   I've had a terrible day. My computer's crashed. The screen is black. The printer's stopped. I can't send e-mail. I've lost my floppy disk and the modem is broken. I'm going home. See you tommorrow.
   Bill

   a. lost — 3. my floppy disk
   b. computer's — 5. crashed
   c. screen is — 1. black
   d. printer's — 6. stopped
   e. can't send — 2. e-mail
   f. modem is — 4. broken

3. **Complete the crossword.**

   1. Have you taken the d____ out of the floppy drive?
   2. My computer's crashed and now it won't s____ .
   3. I want to buy a new p____ . This one is old.
   4. Have you c____ the connection?
   5. My computer had a problem so I t____ it off for a few minutes.
   6. This m____ is too small. I want one with a bigger screen.
   7. This m____ is not fast enough. It takes too long to connect to the Internet.

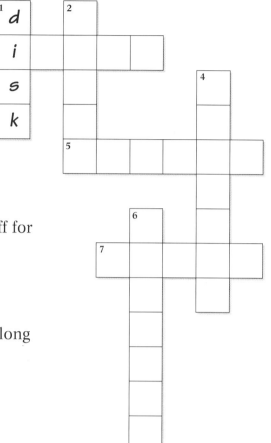

4. 🎧 **Practice your pronunciation. Listen and repeat these sentences. Listen for the stressed words.**

   I've <u>never</u> <u>been</u> to <u>France</u>.
   My com<u>put</u>er's <u>crashed</u>.
   I <u>can't</u> send an <u>e</u>-mail.
   I'<u>ve</u> been <u>scu</u>ba diving.

WORD WATCH PLUS

5. **Match the words on the left with the ones on the right.**

   a. web   1. on
   b. download   2. some software
   c. home   3. engine
   d. surf   4. address
   e. search   5. page
   f. log   6. the Internet

45

12A Have you bought your tickets yet?

1. **Complete the conversation using the phrases below.**

   ~~have you gotten~~   Have you packed   Have you found
   I've been   you've never been

   Mom: Now, Jim, a) ......*have you gotten*...... your plane ticket yet?
   Jim: Yes, Mom. I got it last month. Relax!
   b) .... on vacation lots of times.
   Mom: No, but c) .... to Malaysia before, and last week you said you couldn't find your passport.
   d) .... it?
   Jim: Yes. It was under the bed.
   Mom: Good. e) .... your suitcase yet?
   Jim: Oh, no! I forgot that!

2. **Look at the conversation again. Complete the questions using the words in brackets. Then check the correct answer.**

   a. *Has Jim gotten his plane ticket* .... yet? (Jim / got / plane ticket)
   Yes ✓   No ☐

   b. .... before? (he / be / on vacation)
   Yes ☐   No ☐

   c. .... before? (he / be / Malaysia)
   Yes ☐   No ☐

   d. .... yet? (he / find / passport)
   Yes ☐   No ☐

   e. .... yet? (he / pack / suitcase)
   Yes ☐   No ☐

3. Match the questions on the left with the answers on the right.

a. Have you called your friends yet?
b. Have you booked the restaurant yet?
c. Has Bob invited Susan to the party yet?
d. Have you sent Jane a birthday card yet?
e. Has Tim fed the dog yet?
f. Have they bought the flowers yet?

1. Yes, I have. I mailed it last night.
2. No, they haven't. They're going to buy them this afternoon.
3. Yes, he has. He gave him some steak.
4. Not yet. I'll call them in a minute.
5. No, he hasn't. They had an argument.
6. Yes, I have. I reserved a table for two.

4. Put the words in the correct order to make sentences. Then make the sentences into questions.

a. yet / job / I / found / haven't / a
   I haven't found a job yet.
   Have you found a job yet?

b. bank / I've / this / the / morning / been / to
   ....
   ....

c. a / bought / new / They / yet / car / haven't
   ....
   ....

d. already / homework / has / Mike / done / his
   ....
   ....

e. a / hasn't / yet / arranged / meeting / Tom
   ....
   ....

f. bought / yet / Tim / wife / flowers / his / hasn't / for
   ....
   ....

12B He's passed his driving test.

1. How are these people feeling? Write the adjectives in the correct place below the picture.

   ~~disappointed~~   thrilled   nervous   upset   surprised   angry

a. ......*disappointed*......   c. ....   e. ....
b. ....   d. ....   f. ....

Match each feeling above to a sentence below.

1. Sam hasn't bought his flowers yet.   ...*a*...
2. Jim has found some money.   ....
3. Kenji's dog has eaten Kenji's jacket.   ....
4. Brian hasn't learned to drive yet.   ....
5. Mr. Smith has met the girl.   ....
6. Alice has broken a wedding present.   ....

2. **Read the letter. How is each person feeling, and why?**

> Dear Sue,
> Hi there! I'm writing to tell you Mark has passed his driving test. He's thrilled. He can drive me to work now, so I'm very relieved that I don't have to go by bus. My brother James is upset because he's had a fight with Samantha and she's annoyed because he hasn't said he's sorry. Oh, and the dog has just eaten Mr. Smith's flowers, so Mr. Smith is very angry. We'll keep the dog inside today, I think!
> Love,
> Jane

a. Mark ....thrilled.... He's passed his driving test.
b. Jane ....
c. James ....
d. Samantha ....
e. Mr. Smith ....

3. **Unscramble the letters to find the adjectives.**

a. sedpirurs ....surprised....   d. lelthdri ....
b. nseuovr ....   e. dpeditanoips ....
c. nnoaedy ....   f. etusp ....

4. **Practice your pronunciation. Listen and repeat these words. Do they begin with /r/ or /l/? Write each word in the correct column.**

~~relieved~~ ~~lottery~~ lights written relaxed love

/r/	/l/
relieved	lottery
....	....
....	....

WORD WATCH PLUS

5. **Write *un-*, *im-*, or *in-* to form the opposite of these adjectives.**

a. ..un.. friendly   c. ...... convenient   e. ...... polite
b. ...... happy   d. ...... comfortable f. ...... patient

Word Watch wordlist

These are the key words that you will find in each B lesson of your Student Book.

Lesson 1B

parade
cards
presents
fireworks
float
lanterns
decorations
firecrackers
traditional clothes
candles
exchange
light
put on
put up

Lesson 2B

curry
ice-cream
noodles
fish
beef
pork
soup
salad
shrimps
chicken
fruit tart
tofu
appetizer
entree
dessert

Lesson 3B

romance
science fiction movie
animated movie
documentary
action movie
horror movie
comedy
scary
exciting
romantic
interesting
funny

Lesson 4B

waterfall
gorge
volcano
long
deep
hot
big
high
desert
river
ocean
hot springs
kilometers
meters
degrees

Lesson 5B

graduate from university
go to school
have a baby
get married
die
be born
retire
fall in love
move to a new apartment
separate from (your) partner
get engaged
get a promotion
fail (your) exams
start a new job
Congratulations!
I'm sorry to hear that.
Good luck!

Lesson 6B

environment
gasoline
garbage
public transportation
recycling center
aluminum cans
glass bottles
paper
plastic bottles

Lesson 7B

spacious
messy
neat
stylish
small
cramped
modern
peaceful
bright
dark
old-fashioned
noisy

Lesson 8B

skirt
sweater
jacket
dress
pants
blouse
fashionable
formal
tight
long
cheap
short
baggy
casual
expensive
old-fashioned

Lesson 9B

exhausted
depressed
have a sunburn
lotion
overweight
have insomnia
stressed
have indigestion
have pimples
have a massage
go on a diet
use skin cream

Lesson 10B

airport
declare (your) duty-free goods
show (your) passport
show (your) boarding card
collect (your) baggage
check in (your) baggage
passport control
check-in counter
customs
baggage claim
bank
embassy
doctor's office
travel agency
get some vaccinations
book a ticket
get a visa
buy some traveler's checks

Lesson 11B

computer
screen
mouse
keyboard
printer
modem
floppy disk drive
monitor
floppy disk
send an e-mail

Lesson 12B

upset
surprised
angry
nervous
annoyed
win the lottery
have an argument
fail (your) driving test
find (your) wallet
relieved
disappointed
thrilled
upset

Macmillan Heinemann English Language Teaching
Between Towns Road, Oxford OX4 3PP
A division of Macmillan Publishers Limited
Companies and representatives throughout the world

ISBN 0 333 79963 1
Text © Miles Craven
Design and illustration © Macmillan Publishers Limited 2001
Heinemann is a registered trademark of Reed Educational and Professional Publishing Limited

First published 2001

All rights reserved; no part of this publication may be reproduced, stored in a retrieval system, transmitted in any form, or by any means, electronic, mechanical, photocopying, recording, or otherwise, without the prior written permission of the publishers

Designed by Glynis Edwards
Illustrated by Kathy Baxendale, Paul Cemmick, Glynis Edwards, Phil Garner, Peter Harper, Shaw Harper, Clyde Pearson, John Richardson, David Till
Cover design by Red Giraffe
Cover photos by Pictor (bottom), Stone (top right), Telegraph Colour Library (top left)

Author's acknowledgements
Miles Craven thanks the staff and students of Nihon University, College of International Relations, for their kindness and support. A big thank you also to all colleagues past and present whose creative comments and ideas have influenced my teaching so much over the years.

Special thanks to Angela Buckingham, Lewis Lansford, Valerie Gossage, Rachel Bladon and Timothy Kiggell.

The authors and publishers would like to thank the following for their assistance in the development of this course (in alphabetical order):

Japan
Jane Alderman, James Baquet, James Boyd, Anthony Brewer, Charles Browne, Peter Cowley, Stephen Crabbe, James Craig, Donald Fountaine, Leonard Fullarton, Robert Gaynor, Robert Gray, James Hill, Ann Jenkins, Kerstin Keller, Paul Kelley, Jo Kirihara, Joanne Leyte, Richard Middleton, Charles Olson, Dawn Paullin, J. Nevitt Reagan, Brett Rockwood, Joe Ruellius, Akiko Saito, Mary Sandcamp, Natasha Starr, Tadakuni Tajiri, Kia Tamaki Harrold, Chris Weaver, Tom Webb, Barbara Wells, Akiko Yoshikawa

also Hiroshi Asano, Stuart Bowie, Takashi Hata, Keiko Saito, Satoshi Saito, Yoshiharu Saito and Hajime Shishido

South Korea
Anthony Banks, Roy Beadle, Fred Blair, Parrish Bryan, Paul Cosgrove, Kirsten Duckett, Scarlet Elliott, Gabriel Hahm, Erica Han, Mimi Harvey, Melanie Hoven, Alan Jay, Kaen 'Jeffrey' Joyler, David Kim, Chris Ko, Dr Jong-Bok Kim, Mallory Leece, Larry Michienzi, John Morgan, Terry Nelson, Phillip O'Neill, Charles Petran, Elizabeth Root, Bill Sardo, Sarah Thawley, Peggy Wollberg

also Jeong Sook Lee, Esther Shim and Andrew Todd

Taiwan
Ye-Ling Chang, Carrie Chen, Chwun-Li 'Michelle' Chen, Robert P. Chen, Chun-Tien Chou, Li-Jung 'Becky' Chuang, Ada Hung, Yu-Su Lan, Li-Yun Lin, Irene Shen, Wei-Non Shu, Fu-Hsing Su, Yu-Hsin Tsai, Yi-Lin Yu

also Pearl Lin and May Wang

Thailand
Geoffrey Blyth, Naraporn Chan-Ocha, Ronald Lee Colvin II, Christopher Crowley, Percy Hales, Paul Humphries, Steve Lawrence, Paul McCleave, Kanittha Navarat, Mark Rodell, Perry Roebuck, Rod Rothwell, Brian Waine

also Andrew Allan, Wilaluk Nararoocha, Thawatchai Pattarawongvisut and Anant Rajitganok

Hong Kong
Steve Maginn and Yiu Hei Kan

The authors and publishers would like to thank the following for permission to reproduce their photographs:
Anthony Blake p43; Acraid p28; Corbis p12; James Davis p16; Rex Features p18; Telegraph Colour Library pp20, 42

Printed in Hong Kong

2003 2002 2001 2000
10 9 8 7 6 5 4 3 2 1